Improve your Grammar

Rachel Bladon

Designed by Isaac Quaye
Illustrated by Kevin Faerber

Educational consultants:
Valerie Munro, Angie Graham and Phillipa Ferst

CONTENTS

Them books or *those books*? *You was* or you *were*? It is often difficult to know how to put your words together correctly, but this book will help you improve your grammar skills. It contains fun puzzles that give you lots of practice, as well as simple explanations and guidelines to help you with tricky grammar points.

What is grammar?

Grammar is the way you use words and put them together into sentences that everyone can understand. The rules of grammar help you build sentences that make sense to other people. They tell you how to put words in the right order and use them correctly.

To use these rules correctly, you need to know about the different types of words that make up our language.

Why is grammar important?

To make yourself completely understood, you need to know the rules about things like word order. Putting things in the wrong place can completely change the meaning of a sentence:

Ann ate the fish.   **The fish ate Ann.**

This book will help you avoid mistakes that could make people misunderstand what you are trying to say.

It will also help you improve your English. In everyday situations (when talking or writing to family or friends), people often say things that are not strictly correct. In formal situations, though, like interviews or exams, it is important to use your language correctly.

Besides, even little mistakes like getting one word wrong can change your meaning:

The owner of the car, which was enormous, polished it proudly.   **The owner of the car, who was enormous, polished it proudly.**

Using this book

On pages 3-7 you can find out about the different types of words that make up our language. Knowing about these will help you understand grammar and use it correctly.

On pages 8-26 there are simple explanations and guidelines to help you with tricky points that people often get wrong. For each double page, read the guidelines first, then test yourself with the puzzles. Try all of these, even ones that look easy. They may make something show up that you have not understood.

This is not a write-in book, so you will need paper and a pen or pencil to write your answers down. You can check your answers on pages 27-31.

Watch out for boxes like this one. They contain guidelines and tests on confusing pairs or groups of words that people often slip up on (such as *to* and *too*).

Changing grammar

English grammar is constantly changing. This is because new ways of saying things become accepted and difficult points that people find hard to follow are forgotten. This book does not deal with difficult areas that few people know about. It concentrates instead on common problems and mistakes that actually make what you write or say seem wrong.

In Britain and America, grammar has developed in different ways, so there are many small differences in the way British and American people speak English. For example: a British person might say, "Have you got a pen?" but an American would say, "Do you have a pen?"

Similarly, people from different parts of one country often speak in slightly different ways, called **dialects**.

Internet link: For a link to a website where you can watch a short movie about nouns and try a quiz, go to **www.usborne-quicklinks.com**

R0405594236

dog funny Nouns and adjectives *Jim lonely*

Here, and on the next four pages, you can learn the names for different types of words and find out about the jobs they do in a sentence. You can test what you have learned by doing the puzzles.

Nouns

A **noun** is a word which names a thing, a place, a person or an animal:

drum   **Egypt**

A noun can be **singular** (when naming one thing, as in *cat*) or **plural** (when naming more than one, as in *cats*).

A noun often has a small introducing word called an **article** (*the*, *a* or *an*) in front. For example: *the* sea, *a* car. Nouns which are names of people (and many that are place names) do not have articles in front. For example: *Katie, France, New York.*

Adjectives

An **adjective** is a describing word. It tells you what a noun is like. For example, it can tell you what something looks like, or how big it is. Numbers can also be adjectives: they tell you how many things are being talked about. Here are some common adjectives: *red, large, excellent, ugly.*

Jumbled nouns

Can you complete this story by unscrambling the jumbled nouns?

(Use the picture clues below to help you.)

Four criminals were arrested yesterday in **Pisar** after they tried to steal the Mona Lisa. Pretending to be **ranclees**, the thieves persuaded museum officials to let them remove the priceless **gnapinit**. However, as they were leaving the building, a **clamponie** recognized them as known villains, and the crooks dropped their loot and ran for it. The museum's revolving **rodos** proved to be more than they had bargained for, though. The doors jammed halfway round, and when a passing police **nav** stopped to investigate, **sodg** were able to surround the trapped villains. They are now firmly locked up in **rosnip**, and the famous picture is back in place ready for the weekend **russitot**.

Pisar   ranclees   gnapinit

clamponie   rodos   nav

sodg   rosnip   russitot

Give and take

Find four nouns and three adjectives in sentences 1 to 4. Then write out sentences A to D, completing them with the nouns and adjectives you have found.

1 **Bangkok is often very busy.**
2 **Sarah ran away screaming.**
3 **A black dog was barking loudly.**
4 **The rusty bicycle finally collapsed.**

A **They had bought the ... old car in ... .**
B **Where is ... today?**
C **Outside the house stood a shiny ... .**
D **I'm too ... to take the ... for a walk today.**

3

Verbs

A **verb** is an action word. It tells you what someone or something is doing. For example: *She is working*. Verbs can also show a state (*We live here, He is ill*).

Verbs are very important. They can turn a meaningless group of words (*lions deer*) into an actual sentence*: *Lions attack deer*.

A verb can also tell you about a past action (*They attacked*) or a future action (*They will attack*). There are different forms, or **tenses**, for talking about past, present and future actions. Verbs also change depending on who or what is doing the action (*I attack, He attacks*).

Subject and Object

The person or thing that does an action is called the **subject**. For example, in the sentence *Tim left the house*, *Tim* is the subject. In *He lives next door*, *He* is the subject.

The person or thing that is affected by the action is called the **object**. There are two kinds of objects. A **direct object** is affected directly by an action (for example, *the letter* in the sentence *Matthew sent the letter*). An **indirect object** is usually the person or thing that receives the direct object. Like: *his sister* in *Matthew sent the letter to his sister*.

Pronouns

A **pronoun** is a word you use to replace a noun. Here are some common ones: *I, me, she, it, we, us, them, mine, his, yours*.

Pronouns make language less repetitive. For example, think of two sentences like these: *The frightened girl peered outside. She saw three men waiting below*. Without the pronoun *she*, you would have to repeat *the frightened girl*, which would sound very clumsy.

To do the puzzles on these pages you may need to look back at some of the things that are explained on page 3.

Pronoun fillers

Some pronouns are missing from the report below. Read it through and then decide which pronoun each number stands for.

A yellow lesser-spotted, flat-billed frogcatcher, previously thought to be extinct, has been spotted in the Ice-pie National Park on the east coast. ..1.. was identified by keen birdwatcher Caesar Lotterfeather. ..2.. said yesterday, "..3.. had been out watching with a couple of friends, and as ..4.. were setting off home, ..1.. walked out right in front of us." Caesar said ..2.. and his friends were amazed to see the bird so near ..5..

"..3..'ve been coming here for twenty years but until now ..3..'ve only ever seen seagulls and the odd tern. ..4.. couldn't believe our eyes when we saw the frogcatcher cleaning its feet right in front of ..6.." Caesar was looking forward to reporting back to his wife. "..7.. is always telling ..8.. that ..3.. am wasting my time watching birds. Now ..3.. can really prove to ..9.. that my hobby's worthwhile."

*For more about sentences, see page 8.

leeps us go they sleeps us go they sleeps us go they

Identity parade

In the list below there are five verbs, five nouns, and five words that can be either. Decide which group each word belongs to. Then fit the words that can be either verbs or nouns into sentences 1 to 5.

scream	follow	window
undo	study	hope
add	desk	wander
write	fly	shirt
climb	drawer	girl

1 My sister is hoping to ... art at college.
2 We managed to ... up onto the ridge of the mountain.
3 Her only ... now is that the train is running late.
4 When the man jumped out from behind the door, she let out a loud ... .
5 Mark swatted the ... that kept buzzing around the room.

Sentence spinner

Each ring of this circle contains a jumbled sentence. Rearrange the words in the rings so that each word is in the section labeled with its grammar name. Now you can find five sentences by reading clockwise around the circle, starting with a pronoun each time.

Which sentence still makes sense when its object and subject are swapped over?

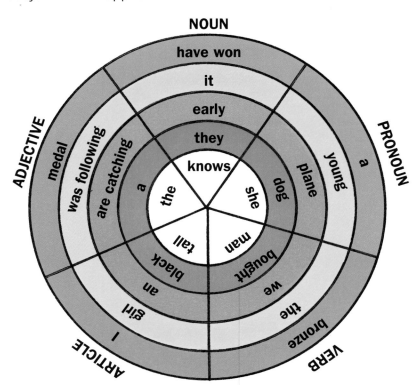

A sack of words

Arrange the words in this sack into five lists, putting all the nouns, verbs, adjectives, pronouns and articles together.

postcard
unhappy sunny will buy
to cry she is working
we an they
the to dream
song
Louise
you
computer waited
loud
beauty a

affect/effect

What is the difference between the words *affect* and *effect*? One is a verb and one is usually a noun, but which is which? Check by looking in a dictionary, then decide which one should go in each of the sentences below.

1 What is the ... of adding flour to water?
2 That movie was really good. There were lots of special ...s.
3 I had a cold, but it didn't really ... me very badly.
4 Her illness had a very bad ... on her test results.
5 The weather can ... the way you feel.

5

Adverbs

An **adverb** is like an adjective, but instead of describing a noun or a pronoun, it tells you more about a verb, an adjective, or even another adverb. An adverb describes how, when or where something happens.

Here are some examples using adverbs: *He smiled <u>politely</u>, Liz drives <u>slowly</u>, We arrived <u>late</u>, Jo lives <u>there</u>, I'm <u>only</u> joking.*

Conjunctions

A **conjunction** is a linking word. It joins other words and groups of words together. Without conjunctions, sentences sound short and jerky. For example: *He closed his eyes. He didn't fall asleep.* The conjunction *but* can turn these into a single sentence: *He closed his eyes, <u>but</u> he didn't fall asleep.*

Here are some common conjunctions: *and, but, or, yet, therefore, so, because, although, while.*

Prepositions

A **preposition** is a word that tells you how one thing is related to another. It is normally attached to a noun or a pronoun.

A lot of prepositions show where one thing is in relation to another. For example: *The dog is lying <u>on</u> the bed.*

Other prepositions show when something happens in relation to something else. For example: *Mike's parents are coming to stay <u>before</u> Christmas.*

Here are some common prepositions: *in, on, under, to, before, after, around, near, down, over, up, past, between, into.*

Lots of verbs look as if they are followed by prepositions (for example, *to break <u>down</u>, to cheer <u>up</u>, to break <u>in</u>*), but in fact, in these cases, these little words are thought of as part of the verb.

Doubling up

Some words can do one job in one sentence, and a different one elsewhere. So, depending on the job they are doing, they can belong to different groups of words. Here are some examples:

1 *Her* and words like *this* and *that* can be pronouns (*Look at <u>her</u>; <u>That</u>'s a pity*) and also adjectives (*It is <u>her</u> jacket; Look at <u>that</u> coat*).

2 Some words, like *hard, late* and *fast,* can be adverbs (*They ran <u>fast</u>; The train arrived <u>late</u>*) or adjectives (*Andy is a <u>fast</u> runner; We are getting a <u>late</u> train*).

3 Words like *so* and *however* can be conjunctions (*He wasn't in, <u>so</u> I left; I am fine, <u>however</u> Jane is not very well*) or adverbs (*I am <u>so</u> tired; <u>However</u> hard he works, he won't pass his exams now*).

Scrambled

Unjumble the prepositions below, then decide which one fits each sentence:

trafe   enetweb   scarso   toni   drune

1   **My car was parked ... the truck and the motorcycle.**
2   **They walked home ... the party.**
3   **The dog jumped ... the lake.**
4   **The prisoner ran as fast as he could ... the bridge.**
5   **The money was hidden ... the bed.**

Internet link: For a link to a website with a useful online guide to different grammar names, go to **www.usborne-quicklinks.com**

ositions   adverbs   conjunctions   prepositions   adverbs

Sentence building

Put these parts of sentences together into the most likely pairs, joining each pair with one of the conjunctions shown in blue.

He couldn't remember her name,

she was jogging.

He forced the door open

crept quietly into the house.

it had already gone.

Michelle rushed to the window and looked for the car,

he had met her before.

my knee hurts.

I can't play tennis today

She listened to music on her headphones

| while | because | but | and | although |

Sentence parts

The sentences below have been split into parts. Write them out, circling each part in the right color to show which grammar group it belongs to.

noun (subject)	article
noun (object)	verb
pronoun (subject)	adverb
pronoun (object)	conjunction
adjective	preposition

1 The / dog / ran / into / the / road / and / the / car / just / missed / it.
2 We / are having / a / big / party, / so / you / must come.
3 The / big / bear / escaped / from / the / zoo / and / was / never / seen / again.
4 The / dancers / were / so / shocked / they / had to stop / the / show.

borrow/lend  *teach/learn*

People often confuse these words. Borrowing is when you take something from someone for a while, but lending is when you give something for a while.

Teaching means showing someone how to do something, or telling them about it. Learning means finding out.

Decide which verb (*borrow*, *lend*, *teach* or *learn*) fits each speech bubble.

Did you ... my shoes again last night?

He is going to ... to speak Spanish before he goes.

Can anyone ... me some money?

She is trying to ... me to sing.

Fill the gap

Choose the correct adjectives or adverbs from the lists below to fill in the gaps in this story. (Use each once only.)

As Ian stepped into the house and wiped his ..1.. shoes on the mat, he heard a ..2.. crash from upstairs. He closed the door ..3.. and waited, trembling. There was no sound. Ian crept across the ..4.. hallway, his heart pounding ..5.. . He tiptoed up the ..6.. stairs, moving ..7.. from one to the next. On the landing, he paused and held his breath. He could just hear a ..8.. sound coming from the sitting room. Ian breathed in ..9.., rested his trembling hand on the door and then ..10.. flung it open. As ..11.. faces appeared all around the room, the lights went on, and a chorus of familiar voices cried ..12.., "Happy Birthday!" Ian sank ..13.. into a chair.

Adjectives: cheerful, loud, muddy, empty, creaky, faint

Adverbs: merrily, thankfully, quietly, deeply, heavily, lightly, suddenly

A sentence is a group of words that makes sense on its own. Most sentences have a subject and a verb. For example: *The cat ran across the garden*. Short exclamations, questions and greetings are also sentences, even though they have no subject or verb. For example: *How amazing! What? Good morning*. A sentence always starts with a capital letter and ends with a period (.), question mark (?) or exclamation point (!).

Clauses and phrases

Sentences can be made up of **clauses** (groups of words that contain verbs) and **phrases** (groups of words without verbs).

A phrase adds extra meaning to a sentence.	A main clause makes sense on its own.

In a panic, she ripped up the letter that he had written.

A subordinate clause depends on a main clause for its meaning. It is usually introduced by a word like *who, which, that, when, where, because, if, although, while* or *before*. Often, though, *who, which* and *that* can be missed out: *In a panic, she ripped up the letter he had written.**

Sentence-building

Sentences come in all shapes and sizes. They can be:

a) **simple**, with only one subject. For example: *The girl wrote a story*.

b) simple, but with adjectives, adverbs and phrases added: *The little girl quickly wrote a funny story about a seahorse*.

c) **compound****, with subordinate clauses and extra main clauses: *The little girl took out her pen, and quickly wrote a funny story about a seahorse which swam across the Atlantic and then drowned in a puddle*.

Keep your sentences short, so that they are absolutely clear. Long, complicated sentences can sound clumsy.

Sentence splitting

The two articles below are each made up of one long, clumsy sentence. Break them both into two by taking out a comma and a conjunction and adding a full stop and a capital letter.

The **Lengthy Express**

BAGGED

Longville mayoress Mrs. Ponsonby-Smythe was in high spirits on Saturday, as she opened the church fête which Longville has been organizing for the past three weeks, but she refused to comment on the incident last week in which local woman Cora Redhanded attacked her with a handbag, accusing her of stealing a bag of flour from her grocery store.

COUCH POTATO KIDS

Children are much less healthy these days, because they spend so much time sitting like couch potatoes in front of the television or playing computer games while they stuff their faces with chips and soda pop, and they don't get much exercise either, because they go everywhere by car or by public transportation, instead of walking.

8
*There is more about this on page 18.
**The word "compound" means "made up of several parts".

Internet link: For a link to a website with factsheets, quizzes and games on sentences, go to **www.usborne-quicklinks.com**

minute *because they knew* *we laughed* *while she danced*

Clause-spotting

Decide whether each group of words below is a main clause, a subordinate clause or a phrase. Put one of each type together to make four sentences, then arrange these into a short story, beginning *In the house next door ...*

In the house next door

in a fast car

which had incredibly long legs.

in a panic

One day he let it out

which squashed the poor stick insect.

while Mrs. Kettani was in her yard.

because she was terrified of large insects.

They arrived

She phoned the police

my friend kept a stick insect

in the street

Sentence stretch

Add an adjective, an adverb and a subordinate clause from the lists below to each of these sentences. (Put the adverb just in front of the verb, and the subordinate clause at the end.)

1 The monkey ate six bananas.

2 She eats at the restaurant.

3 He drove the car into a ditch.

4 Joanna walked up to the horse.

Adjectives: hungry, young, new, Chinese.

Adverbs: stupidly, slowly, greedily, often.

Subordinate clauses:
where her brother is a waiter.
which had thrown her off its back.
when the zookeeper had gone.
because he was fiddling with the radio.

an/a

an usually goes in front of:

a) words that begin with a vowel (*a, e, i, o* or *u*)
   egg, apple

b) words beginning with a letter such as *h* when it sounds like a vowel
   hour, heir

c) single letters (often in sets of initials) that sound like vowels
   SOS (*S* is said as "ess")
   MP (*M* is said as "em")

a usually goes in front of:

a) words that begin with a consonant (a letter that is not a vowel)
   door, book, clock

b) words beginning with vowels that sound like consonants
   university, European (both begin with "yuh" sounds)
   one-way street begins with a "wuh" sound)

Add either *an* or *a* to each of these nine sentences:

1 He gave me ... used railway ticket.

2 Jill said she had seen ... UFO.

3 They gave her ... X-ray and said she'd be fine.

4 From his window he has ... incredible view over New York.

5 This is ... one-way street.

6 Sometimes, a friend can turn into ... enemy.

7 It was such ... hot day.

8 It was ... honest answer.

9 He has ... older brother.

On these two pages you can find some useful hints on how to arrange words so that your sentences are as clear as possible.

Keeping together

Words that are connected to each other should always be kept together in a sentence. Here are two rules to help you with this:

1 Try to keep the subject and the verb as close together as possible, especially in long sentences. For example: _Jim read the letter one last time, while Emma went to the phone and called the police._

The meaning can be unclear if the subject and the verb are far apart: _Jim, while Emma went to the phone and called the police, read the letter one last time._

2 Phrases and subordinate clauses should go as near as possible to the words they refer to.

If you put them in the wrong place, your sentence may sound very strange. For example: _The farmer rounded up the sheep that had run away with the sheepdog's help._

Moving the phrase _with the sheepdog's help_ nearer to _the farmer_ makes the meaning clear: _With the sheepdog's help, the farmer rounded up the sheep that had run away._

Shifting adverbs

Certain adverbs, like _only_ and _just_, give sentences a slightly different meaning, depending on their position. You should normally put them in front of what they refer to, as shown here:

I told only Christopher that I had won second prize. (Christopher was the only person I told.)

I only told Christopher that I had won second prize. (It was the only thing I told him.)

I told Christopher that I had only won second prize. (I told him I had only won second prize, not first.)

Split infinitives

The **infinitive** of a verb (_to_ plus the verb, as in _to go, to work, to drive_) is its most basic form. You should avoid breaking up (or splitting) the two parts of the infinitive, particularly if you are writing formally or any time it sounds awkward. Thus, _to boldly go_ would be better phrased as _to go boldly_ or _boldly to go._

Splitting up

Sarah's family are going away for the week. Spot the split infinitives in the notes they have left, then move the words that are splitting them to the end of the sentences.

You can finish all the food in the freezer, except for the chocolate cake I made for Dad's birthday, and the leg of lamb, which I'd like you to please take out on Saturday. Also, before Mr. Hopkins drops by on Wednesday, I'd like you to thoroughly vacuum the sitting room.

Before you go out, remember to carefully double-lock the door.

Please don't forget to put Bingo out before you go to bed. You need to every night feed my goldfish.

Could you remember to regularly water the tomatoes? By the way, I told Mary you'd try to quickly drop in on her.

See you on Saturday - we're going to if possible try to get the afternoon train. Perhaps you could pick us up from the station if we give you a call?

23 123 123 123 123 123 123 123 123 123

Picture puzzlers

Next to each pair of pictures below, there is a short sentence, and one phrase or clause (in yellow). Make two new sentences (one to match each picture) by inserting this phrase or clause in two different places in the sentence*.

1 **The girl gave the envelope to the man.**
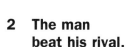

2 **The man beat his rival.**
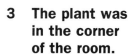

3 **The plant was in the corner of the room.**

4 **Jane rested her foot on the top rung of the ladder.**
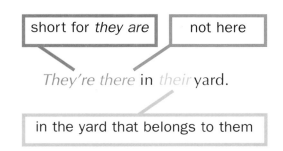

Adverb adding

Write out sentence 1 three times, putting the adverb *just* in a different place each time, so that the sentences have the meanings given in A, B and C.

Then do the same with sentence 2, using the adverb *only*.

Sentence 1: He's told me I will have to take it easy for a few days.
A **He told me a minute ago.**
B **The only thing I have to do is take it easy.**
C **I have to take it easy, but only for a few days.**

Sentence 2: There were a few chocolates left, but Sue ate two.
A **There weren't many chocolates, but Sue took two anyway.**
B **There were some chocolates left, but Sue only took two.**
C **There were some chocolates left, but Sue was the only person who took two.**

🍌 *their/they're/there*

Because they sound the same, it is easy to get *their, they're* and *there* mixed up. Here you can see the different meanings of these words:

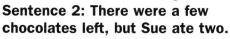

There is also used with *to be* to say things like *there is* (or *there's*) and *there are*.

For sentences 1 to 6, which word or group of words in brackets fits the gap?

1 **There ... in a netball team.**
   (daughter is/all/are seven people)
2 **Their ... outside.**
   (are two men/dog is/waiting)
3 **They're ... in the swimming pool.**
   (still/dog is/we were)
4 **Their ... way.**
   (lawyer is on his/is a tree in the/on their)
5 **Isn't she there ...?**
   (new teacher/any more)
6 **They're ... on vacation.**
   (friend is/were two of us/away)

*You may need to add commas to make the meaning clear. See page 18.

Simple agreements

Always make sure that the subject agrees with (matches) the verb. Here you can see what this means:

singular subject	verb must be singular

Sarah is out,
but *the twins are* upstairs.

plural subject	verb must be plural

Tricky cases

Sometimes it is difficult to know whether to use a singular or plural verb with the subject. Here are some hints to help you:

1 The words *anyone, everyone, no one* and *each* are always followed by a singular verb. For example: *Everyone is asleep.*

The words *many, both, (a) few* and *several* are always followed by a plural verb. For example: *Several are missing.*

2 When the subject is two words joined by *and* (as in *Annie and her friend*), you use a plural verb: *Here come Annie and her friend.*

3 When the subject is a group of words, such as *members of the gang*, the verb must agree with the actual word it relates to:

These members of the gang are the toughest.

verb relates to this word (the *members* are the toughest, not the *gang*)	verb is plural to match *members*

4 Singular words which name groups of people (like *family, team* or *school*) can be used with either singular or plural verbs.

To talk about the group as a whole, you normally use a singular verb: *Each team has three turns.* To talk about it as a group of members, you can use a plural verb: *The team were excited about the match.*

Island mission

Agent Craxitall is on the trail of the notorious criminal, Ivor Cunningplan. He has discovered some pieces of the torn-up instructions for Ivor's latest mission. Fit them together to find out what Ivor has to do and where he is heading.

IF SOMEONE SAYS: "HERE COMES

FIVE MEMBERS OF THE GANG

TRACKHAM DOWN DETECTIVES

CODE NAME: CRAXITALL AGENT 008

KNOWS THAT THE DOCUMENTS ARE BEING DELIVERED BY A MAN WITH A LIMP.

LIE IN THE WYLIN OCEAN.

YOUR MISSION IS TO DELIVER THE SILICON DOCUMENTS TO THE LEADER OF THE SNEAK STREET GANG.

FIRST GO TO THE ISLANDS OF SKEE-MING, WHICH

THEN HEAD FOR THE CITY OF SKA-LEE-WAGS, WHICH

ONCE THERE, YOU WILL EASILY LOCATE SNEAK STREET. ON FRIDAY NIGHT,

ART FULFOX AND HIS DOG," THEN IT IS NOT SAFE TO DELIVER THE DOCUMENTS.

EACH MEMBER

ARE MEETING ON THE CORNER OF SNEAK STREET.

WALK UP TO THE GANG. IF SOMEONE SAYS: "HERE COME

IS ON THE NORTHERNMOST ISLAND.

ART FULFOX," YOU CAN DROP THEM OFF AND RETURN TO HQ.

e *everyone* is *both are* *it is* *they are* *everyone* is *both are*

Beach breaks

In this game, each white space shows the first half of a sentence. Starting at the blue arrow, move around from space to space, following the direction of the footprint containing the matching half sentence. You must go through all the white spaces before taking a red exit. Which exit, A to G, will you take?

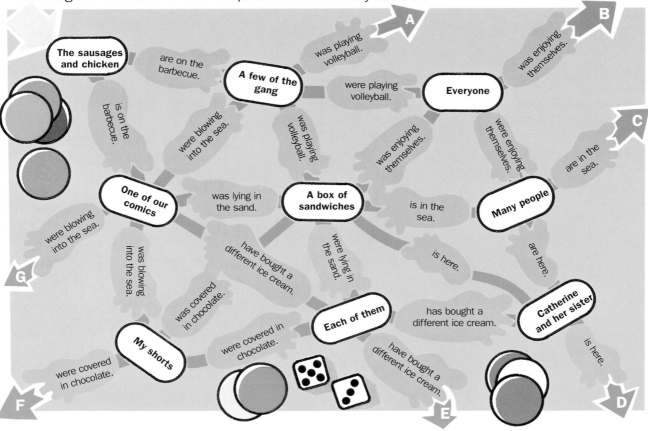

off/of

Off is nearly always connected to a verb. It can be a preposition (*They dropped it off the bridge*) or part of a verb (*They got off at the bus stop*).

Of is normally used after adjectives (as in *afraid of*), or after words that show quantity or numbers of things (as in *a few of, some of, a piece of, lots of*).

Of is sometimes used with a verb. In these cases, it often means *about* (for example, *to dream of, to think of*).

Which of these sentences is missing *off*, and which is missing *of*?

1 He is very proud ... his polar bear costume.
2 Kathy stopped ... in Zambia on her way to Swaziland.
3 Her brother reminds me ... a chimpanzee.
4 Most ... the chocolate fudge cake had already been eaten.
5 As she was getting ... the train, she saw the man.
6 Vicky has always been terrified ... cats.
7 The plane took ... late.

Fill the gaps

Fit one of the yellow words below into each sentence.

1 There ... layers of dust on the piano.
2 "Here ... Ann and Graham!" she shrieked, pointing across the street.
3 A little bit of money ... a long way.
4 When we got back, there ... a bucketful of tomatoes on the doorstep.
5 Most motorbikes are cheaper than cars and ... much faster.
6 Success ... more important to him than happiness.

is was go were are goes

13

Verbs have different forms for talking about the past, the present and the future. For example:

I worked, *I am working*, *I will work*. These different verb forms are called **tenses**.

Tenses Here you can see the main tenses. The examples, using the verb *to wait*, show how they are formed for most verbs.

PAST			PRESENT	FUTURE
past perfect	past simple*	present perfect	present simple*	future
had waited	*waited*	*have/has waited*	*wait/waits*	*shall/will wait*

For many common verbs, the past tenses are irregular (not formed in the way shown here). There is a list of common irregular verbs on page 16.

Many of these tenses also have **continuous** forms, such as the present continuous (I *am waiting*), and past continuous (I *was waiting*). These are normally used for something that is, was or will already be happening at a particular time.

There are other ways of talking about the future. For example, to talk about plans or things you intend to do, you can use *going to* with the verb (as in *Tomorrow I am going to write* to my parents).

Showing order

To talk about several things that happened at different times, you show the order they happened in by using different tenses. For example, when you use the past simple to talk about things that happened in the past, you can use the past perfect to show an action that took place even further back in time:

happened second	**happened first (a while ago)**

He *walked up* to the man who *had won*, and as he *handed* him the gleaming gold medal, he *said*, "Soon you *will be* famous."

both happened third (just after what happened second)	**will happen fourth**

When talking about a set of events, be careful not to jump from one tense to another (unless you are talking about things that happened at different times). Look at the example below.

She rushed downstairs, opened the door and <u>picks</u> up the parcel which the mailman had delivered. — **This should say <u>picked</u>.**

 *like/as*

You use *like* and *as* to compare things. Like goes in front of a noun or a pronoun. For example: *She is <u>like</u> her father.*

As goes in front of a clause (which has a subject and a verb). For example: *Everything was just <u>as</u> he had left it.*

As is also used in many other expressions which compare things in some way: *<u>as</u> if, <u>as</u> good as, <u>as</u> usual, <u>as</u> before.*

Make six sentences by joining a first half (on the left) with a second half (on the right), using *like*, *as* or *as if*.

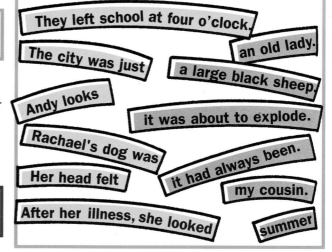

They left school at four o'clock.
The city was just
an old lady.
a large black sheep.
Andy looks
it was about to explode.
Rachael's dog was
it had always been.
Her head felt
my cousin.
After her illness, she looked
summer

*In negative sentences (ones that use *not*) and in questions, use *did* with the past simple (*Did I wait?*) and *do/does* with the present simple (*He does not wait*).

Internet link: For a link to a website with a quiz on choosing the correct tense, go to www.usborne-quicklinks.com

ile *walked* *is walking* *will walk* *smiled* *is smiling*

Tense trippers

Louise has kept a diary of the cycling trip she went on with some friends, but she has put twelve verbs in the wrong tense. Can you correct her mistakes?

Monday
Just before lunch Stuart got a flat tire. No one had a flat tire repair kit, so we have to walk miles to the nearest town. When we finally got there, someone directed us to a bike shop, so we go all the way there and then find it was closed.

Tuesday
The day went well until we get caught behind a herd of sheep on a narrow lane. It took us two hours to get past them, so by the time we got to the youth hostel, it's completely full.

Wednesday
Stopped for lunch in a little village. Left our bikes by the church, went to a café, and when we come out, Sheila's bike has disappeared. Then suddenly we spotted the local priest riding the missing bike, so we flag him down and he explained everything. The poor priest sold his own bike a year ago, but he keeps forgetting, so every time he sees a black bike he thought it's his.

Thursday
Arrived at the station to get the train home. We loaded our bikes on board and then go for coffee while we are waiting. Suddenly, Stuart noticed that the train was leaving! We put our bikes on the wrong one!

Which is which?

Copy the list of verbs below. Then decide which tenses they are in, and underline each one as shown here:

past perfect
past simple
present perfect
present simple
future

have crashed
smiled
had promised
sit
had visited
will understand
did not arrive
buys
has spotted
will drive
invaded
sing
had painted

Getting snappy

Louise wanted to arrange her photos in the order in which they were taken, but she has mixed them up.

For each caption (A, B, C and D), write out the numbers of the photos in the order she should arrange them.

A **At a local market, we met the boy who had fixed Stuart's bike, so we all went to the fair together.**

B **Every morning, fishermen in this village sell fresh fish that they have caught from their boats. By lunchtime, they will have none left.**

C **After we'd spotted the priest riding the bike Sheila had left outside the church, we all went for coffee together.**

D **On Tuesday, we had a picnic, and then went for a swim in a little cove we'd read about the night before.**

Hints

These hints will help you decide which tenses to use in long sentences:

1 When the verb in the main clause is in the past tense (as in *I was mad*), the verbs in the subordinate clauses usually go into a past tense as well (*I was mad because he had not locked the door*).

2 When the verb in the main clause is in the future (*We will go*), or has a future meaning, verbs in the subordinate clauses usually go into the present (*We will go when he arrives*).

Which past tense?

You use the **past simple** to talk about something that happened at a particular time (as in *She arrived yesterday*).

You use the **present perfect** when it is not important to know exactly when something happened (*I have been to Egypt*), or when something is still going on (*I have lived here for two years*).

The present perfect is made using *has* or *have* and the **past participle**. For most verbs, the past participle is exactly like the past simple (*I called, I have called*).

The past participle is also used with *had* to form the **past perfect** (*I had called*). There is more about forming tenses on page 14.

Irregulars

Some common verbs have past simples and past participles that are **irregular**. This means they are not formed in the usual way (by adding *ed*). Here you can see a few tricky ones:

verb	past simple	past participle
to be	was/were*	been
to begin	began	begun
to break	broke	broken
to do	did	done
to drink	drank	drunk
to eat	ate	eaten
to forget	forgot	forgotten
to give	gave	given
to go	went	gone/been**
to run	ran	run
to sing	sang	sung
to swim	swam	swum
to take	took	taken

Can you think of any more verbs that have irregular past simples or past participles? You will need to know some others to do all the puzzles on these pages.

―――――――――― **Lost for words** ――――――――――

Which word from the yellow list below fits which speech bubble?

I have ... too much ice cream.

I ... a lot of ice cream when I was in Italy.

I have just ... my sister's sunglasses.

Last week I ... Mr. Bailey's window.

I ... in the bathtub this morning.

I have just ... across the lake.

I ... across it yesterday.

I have ... all my homework.

Nicky ... hers last week.

broke/broken/ swum/swam/ eaten/ate/ sang/done/did

*Use *was* with *I, he, she* and *it,* and *were* with *you, we* and *they.*
**Use *gone* when the subject is still away, and *been* when they have already returned.

ng   *have rung   did   have done   swam   has swum*

Andrew's desk

Picture A shows what was on Andrew's desk one morning, and picture B shows what was there in the evening. Choosing verbs from the list below, write four sentences (beginning each one *He has ...*) to show what Andrew has done at his desk during the day.

Then rewrite these sentences, using the past simple. Begin each one *In the afternoon, ...*

to blow out, to break, to eat, to write

Tense trouble

Spot which verb is in the wrong tense in each of the sentences below.

1 They will have to pick up the house before their parents will get back.
2 Oliver had just finished writing when the examiner tells them to put down their pens.
3 Lots of people visit the exhibition when it opens next month.
4 I was furious because the train has been late.
5 She has been to Hong Kong last year.
6 They lived in New York for six years, and have no plans to move away.

can/may/might

Here you can see when to use *can*, *may* and *might*:

	can	may	might
1 Talking about something that is possible	use *can* to talk about something that you are able to do: *I can swim.*	use *may* for something that is possible and quite likely: *I may go for a swim.*	use *might* for something that is possible but not so likely: *I might go for a swim.*
2 Asking for permission	To ask permission or to give it, you can use *can* or *may*. *May* is more grammatically correct though, so you should use it in formal situations: *May I go home?* or *You may leave.* Use *can* in less formal situations: *Can I have a cookie?* or *You can have two chocolates.*		*might* is sometimes used in very formal situations: *Might I ask a question?*
3 Giving permission			never use *might*

Decide which word, *may*, *might* or *can* should fill the gaps in these sentences:

1 I am very glad that Jenny ... speak French.
2 You ... spend as much money as you like.
3 ... I borrow a pencil? (talking to a friend)
4 ... I phone my parents? (talking to someone you don't know)
5 I ... go and see a movie this afternoon, if it keeps on raining.

17

Could is often used instead of *can* to ask for permission. It is less direct (and more polite) than *can*.

Which, that, who, whom and *whose* are called **relative pronouns**. They usually introduce clauses which tell you more about a noun. For example: *There are those awful people who live at number 6*.

Different clauses

Relative pronouns work in different ways, depending on whether they are introducing a restrictive or a non-restrictive clause.

A **restrictive clause** spells out who or what the noun is, as in *There is the dog which bit my rabbit*.

A **non-restrictive clause** simply tells you more about a noun whose identity is already clear. Think of it as the part of the sentence that could go in parentheses. For example: *Mr. Parker's dog, which bit my rabbit, has just attacked the milkman*.

When speaking, you do not often use non-restrictive clauses. They are always split off from the rest of the sentence by commas, but restrictive clauses are not.

Relative pronouns

Here you can see which relative pronoun to use, depending on whether you are talking about a person or a thing*:

RESTRICTIVE CLAUSES

for people	*who (or whom)/that*
for things	*which/that*

1 That can often replace who or which (as in the man that stole the bananas).
2 You can often leave out the relative pronoun altogether: That is the dog (which) I rescued.

NON-RESTRICTIVE CLAUSES

for people	*who (or whom)*
for things	*which*

1 You cannot use that instead of who or which.
2 You cannot leave out the relative pronoun.

Whom, whose

Whom can stand for a person, if that person is the object** of the clause (as in *That is the doctor whom I saw*). In spoken English, it is normally replaced with *who* or *that*.

Whose stands for someone to whom something belongs (*The man whose car I had hit chased me*).

Prepositions

After a preposition (see page 6), you use *whom* instead of *who*, and *which* instead of *that*. For example: *the man to whom I gave my ticket*. It is often easier, though, to turn the clause around and leave out the relative pronoun: *the man I gave my ticket to*.

Identity crisis

Rewrite the sentences below, removing any non-restrictive clauses.

1 The fridge is full of bacon, which I eat every day.
2 The ring which he gave me was far too big.
3 The policeman who drove them home was very friendly.
4 My brother, who is a vet, is getting married.
5 The boat, which was found by a diver, had been underwater for thirty years.

Who or *whom?*

Write out these sentences, completing two with *who* and two with *whom*.

1 The friend with ... I went to Egypt has sent me a letter.
2 The people ... took the other path got there first.
3 Valerie, ... has just come back from Mexico, speaks fluent Spanish.
4 This is Jo, ... I met on a bus.

18
*For an animal, depending on how you think of it, you can either follow the pattern for people or for things.
**Remember, the subject does the action and the object has the action done to it.

which *that* *who* *whom* *whose* *which* *that* *who* *whom*

Murder at Snoot Towers

Read this report on the murder of Lord Snoot, and decide which relative pronoun (below) should go in each space. Then use the plan of Snoot Towers to identify the most likely murderer.

Lord Snoot's body, ..1.. was found in the conservatory, was identified by his widow. Lady Snoot, ..2.. will inherit several million dollars from her husband, was in the drawing room with the gardener at the time of the murder, looking at designs for a sunken garden ..3.. she wanted installed. Hugo Batty, ..4.. knew the truth about Snoot's business affairs, and to ..5.. Snoot had just given six thousand dollars, was working in the library. Will Snoot, ..6.. fiancée was lunching with his sister in the dining room (both women are eliminated from the inquiry), was shooting grouse in Snoot Forest. Lord Snoot had earlier forbidden him to marry his fiancée. The cook and the butler were in the pantry, ..7.. can only be reached from the drawing room. They said they heard Lord Snoot's cousin, Earl Toffeenose, talking in the billiard room with the nanny, ..8.. Snoot had just fired. Nobody passed through any of the rooms ..9.. anyone else was in around the time of the murder.

that/which
whom
who
which
whose
which
whom/that
that
who

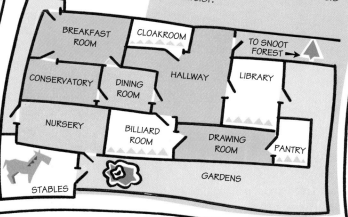

BREAKFAST ROOM | CLOAKROOM | TO SNOOT FOREST →
CONSERVATORY | DINING ROOM | HALLWAY | LIBRARY
NURSERY | BILLIARD ROOM | DRAWING ROOM | PANTRY
STABLES | GARDENS

of/'ve

In speech, *have* is often shortened to *'ve* after *should, would, may, must, might* and so on. For example: *You should've gone.**

Be careful not to confuse *'ve* with *of*, which sounds very similar. Never use *of* instead of *have* with the words listed above.

Complete these pieces of conversation with *should've, would've, could've* and *must've*. (Use each once only.)

1 "She ... decided not to take her car, because I saw it parked in our street this morning."
2 "You really ... gone to the party: it was great fun."
3 "We ... driven a bit faster, but not much, as the roads are very wet."
4 "If it hadn't been raining, I ... come."

Who's who and what's what?

Look at the pictures, then decide which clause from the list on the right fits which sentence best. (Use each once only.)

1 The girl ... is near the boat.
2 The dog ... has black paws.
3 The ice cream ... is chocolate and vanilla.
4 The boy ... has red hair.
5 The cow ... has black ears.
6 The dog ... is near the boat.
7 The baby ... has a pink hat.
8 The man ... has a red sweater.

THE POLICEMAN IS CHASING
WHICH IS SWIMMING
WHICH THE BOY IS HOLDING
WHICH IS RUNNING
WHO IS SWIMMING
WHOM THE POLICEMAN IS CHASING
WHO IS RUNNING
THE WOMAN IS HOLDING

*When writing, you should normally use *have*, not *'ve.*

Comparatives and superlatives

Comparatives and superlatives are special forms of adjectives that are used for comparing things.

You use a **comparative** (such as *taller, more intelligent*) to compare people or things with each other.
For example: *Simon is <u>taller</u> than Andrew and Tim.*

You use a **superlative** (such as *the tallest, the most intelligent*) to show that one thing stands out above all the rest. For example: *Simon is <u>the tallest</u> in the class.*

Different forms

Most comparatives are made either by adding *er* to the adjective, or putting *more* in front of it. Most superlatives are made by adding *est* or putting *the most* in front.

The form you use depends on how many syllables the adjective has. A **syllable** is part of a word that contains a vowel sound. For example, *lazy* has two syllables containing the vowel sounds "ay" and "ee".

Here are some general rules on which form to use. Examples are shown in blue:

ADJECTIVE	COMPARATIVE	SUPERLATIVE
one-syllable adjective* *hard*	*-er* *harder*	*the -est* *the hardest*
one-syllable adjective ending in *e* *white*	*-r* *whiter*	*the -st* *the whitest*
adjective with two or more syllables *careful*	*more ...* *more careful*	*the most ...* *the most careful*
two-syllable adjective ending in *y* *funny*	*-er* (and change *y* to *i*) *funnier*	*the -est* (and change *y* to *i*) *the funniest*

The important thing to remember is that you either add *er* (or *est*) OR use *more* (or *the most*). Never do both.

Irregulars

Here are some common adjectives which have irregular comparatives and superlatives:

ADJECTIVE	COMPARATIVE	SUPERLATIVE
good	*better*	*the best*
bad	*worse*	*the worst*
much/many	*more*	*the most*
little	*less*	*the least*

Adverbs, I/me

Adverbs also have comparative and superlative forms. These work just as for adjectives, except that for most long adverbs ending in y, you use *more/the most* instead of adding *er/est*.

It is common to use *me, him, her, us* and *them* after a comparative with *than* (as in *He is older than <u>me</u>*). In formal situations, though, people sometimes use *I, he, she, we* and *they* (*He is older than I*).

— Comparing climates —

Look at these charts of the temperature and total rainfall for two cities through the year. Then write out the sentences below, adding comparatives of *hot, cold* (for 1 and 2), *wet* and *dry* (for 3 and 4).

1 **In August, Weatherchester is ... than Seasonbury.**
2 **In January, Weatherchester is ... than Seasonbury.**
3 **In March, Seasonbury is ... than Weatherchester.**
4 **In September, Seasonbury is ... than Weatherchester.**

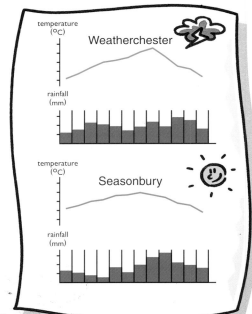

*For adjectives ending in *y* (such as *dry*), you change *y* to *i* (*drier, the driest*). For those ending in one vowel and one consonant (such as *hot*), you double the consonant (*hotter, the hottest*).

Internet link: For a link to a website where you can see if you can correct the words used for comparing things, go to **www.usborne-quicklinks.com**

Character questionnaire

Jon and Tessa have done a magazine quiz, each of them putting their initial by the answer they have chosen. Based on their answers, and making comparatives from the adjectives on the list, write six sentences comparing Jon and Tessa. For example: *Jon is taller than Tessa.*

Quiz

nosy
selfish
lazy
friendly
patient
careful

1 You have been waiting for a bus for half an hour. You:

a) wait patiently, feeling glad you are not in a hurry. **J**

b) pace up and down, looking at your watch. **T**

c) decide to walk - the exercise will do you good.

2 Arriving home, you realize you have forgotten to mail an urgent letter for your mother. You:

a) pretend to have forgotten all about it until it is too late. **J**

b) ask your brother to mail it on his way to football practice.

c) go straight out to mail it before you forget again. **T**

3 There is a new girl in your class, and at lunchtime you notice her sitting on her own. You:

a) ask her to come and join you and your friends. **T**

b) make a point of talking to her later on.

c) ignore her. **J**

4 You are walking a friend's dog in the countryside. You:

a) put it on the leash every time you see a road ahead. **J**

b) keep an eye on it whenever you are on a road.

c) let it wander ahead - after all, the roads are very quiet. **T**

5 You hear your sister on the phone and she is clearly upset. You:

a) strain your ears to listen in. **T**

b) hum loudly, so you can't hear anything. **J**

c) listen in, then ask her later on what was wrong.

6 For your birthday you are given a small box of chocolates. You:

a) guzzle them in your room rather than share them. **J**

b) offer them around once, then eat the rest yourself.

c) offer them to all your friends, leaving none for yourself. **T**

quite/quiet

People often confuse these words. *Quite* is an adverb that either means "very" (as in *I'm quite tired*), or "completely" (*I'm quite lost*). *Quiet* is an adjective that means the opposite of "noisy"/"loud".

Passed and *past* are also confusing. *Passed* can only be used as a verb (as in *He passed the salt*). *Past* can be used as an adjective (*the past year*), a noun (*He lives in the past*), a preposition (*She ran past me*) or an adverb (*A gull flew past*).

Write these sentences out, adding *quite, quiet, passed* or *past*.

1 You look ... washed out.
2 As Stefan walked ..., he noticed the man's gun.
3 It is very ... without Diane and Vicky.
4 Veronica was so happy when she ... her test.
5 In the ... week, I have lost two umbrellas.
6 I have always found math ... hard.

Moped mania

Sally is not sure which moped to buy. Using the table on the right, and the adjectives *wide, long, expensive, fast* and *heavy*, write five sentences to compare the Superwhizz and the Pipsqueak.

Then do the same for the Stumbly and the Featherzoom, and for the Pipsqueak and the Thriftyshift.

Sally can only spend $4000, and the space in her garage is 3 x 10 feet. Which is the fastest moped she can buy?

Moped	Width (feet)	Length (feet)	Price ($)	Top speed (miles per hour)	Weight (lbs)
Superwhizz	3	9.5	4500	65	95
Pipsqueak	2	8	3800	50	75
Stumbly	3.5	9.5	3000	40	80
Featherzoom	3	11	3400	60	65
Thriftyshift	2.5	10	2000	45	70

Conditional sentences are used to talk about things that can only happen under certain conditions*. For example: *If he said he was sorry, I would forgive him.*

There are three main types. They are made up of two clauses, each in a different tense, one of which is introduced by *if*. Most contain a verb in the **conditional** (such as *would go*) or **conditional perfect** (*would have gone*).

Type 1

if clause in present tense	other clause in future tense

"If I win an Olympic medal,
I will give all the prize money to charity."

This type is used to talk about something that is likely to happen. In the example, the person speaking has a good chance of winning an Olympic medal.

Type 2

if clause in past tense	other clause in conditional

"If I won an Olympic medal,
I would give all the prize money to charity."

This type is used to talk about something that is unlikely to happen. In the example, the person speaking is just imagining what it would be like to win an Olympic medal.

Type 3

if clause in past perfect	other clause in conditional perfect

"If I had won an Olympic medal,
I would have given all the prize money to charity."

This type is used to imagine what would have been possible if things had turned out differently. In the example, the person speaking entered the Olympics, but did not win a medal.

Always remember that the conditional perfect does not go in the *if* clause. This means it is wrong to say things like *if I'd have had*.

Was/were, should
In formal situations, you should use *were*** instead of *was*** after *if*. This is especially true when you are giving advice. For example: *If I <u>were</u> you, I wouldn't do that.*
    You can use *should* instead of *would* when the subject is *I* or *we*. For example: *If I were you, I <u>should</u> stay at home.*

 in/into

To show that something moves from one place to another, use *into*, especially after the verbs *go, come, walk* and *run*. For example: *Ellie ran <u>into</u> the room.*
    To show that something stays in the same place, use *in* (*It is <u>in</u> the corner*).
    Lots of verbs can be used with either *in* or *into*, but stick to the rules given above and you will always be right.

Add *in* or *into* to each of these sentences:

1 **He could see a girl diving ... the pool.**
2 **Elaine hurried ... her bedroom.**
3 **The train had been waiting ... the tunnel for more than half an hour.**
4 **We went ... the garden to look for worms.**
5 **I lay ... the bathtub for forty minutes today.**

When you talk about facts, rather than conditions, you don't need the conditional tense. For example: If you heat ice, it melts.
**These are forms of the verb *to be*.

Internet link: For a link to a website with an exercise about verb tenses in conditional sentences, go to **www.usborne-quicklinks.com**

e would leave   *if I had*   I would know   he would leave

Split conditionals

Here you can see six sentences which have each been split in two. Put them back together again and match each sentence with the correct picture.

they would not have died.

If I water the plants,

I will bite her.

I would have won.

I will win.

If she had pulled my ear,

I would have bitten her.

If she pulls my ear,

If I had watered the plants,

they will not die.

If I run faster,

If I had run faster,

Dear Maisie

Look at this magazine problem page. Can you replace each number with the correct form of one of the verbs shown here?

to think/to pass/to stop/to be/ to have to/to speak/to eat

HELP!

Dear Maisie,
I failed all my finals again this semester, and my teacher says that if I don't work harder, I ..1.. leave the school. But I just can't concentrate.

Switch the TV off and put those magazines away. If you ..2.. your exams the first time, you wouldn't have had these problems.

Dear Maisie,
I want to become a vegetarian, but my mother says if I ..3.. eating meat I will be sick.

Your mother is right to be concerned, but if you ..4.. lots of protein foods you will not be ill.

Dear Maisie,
I have an enormous pimple on the end of my nose. I've tried everything, but I just can't get rid of it.

If I ..5.. you, I would try some Wondersqueeze cream. It never fails!

Dear Maisie,
I want to join a tennis club, but I'm very shy. If anyone ..6.. to me, I would turn bright red and start shaking.

In that case, you should definitely join a tennis club. If you do turn red and start shaking, no one ..7.. it is odd: lots of people are very shy.

A wobbly welcome

Barry, the Boppa Breaks tourist guide, has written a welcome note for tourists arriving in Costa Boppa. He has circled a few mistakes that he has made, but is not sure how to correct them. Can you make the necessary corrections?

Hi folks! Welcome to Costa Boppa! This is the world's most remote island: if you (came) by boat it would have taken you thirty-nine hours to get here. But it's also the world's most happening hotspot: if you went to the Costa Brava you (will not find) wilder nightlife.

Costa Boppa is simply gorgeous. If you got up at four o'clock, you (would have seen) some amazing sunrises. If you (wanted) to explore the island a bit, your Boppa Breaks guide will be happy to arrange a bus tour and cultural extravaganza.

If you come on down to the Boppa Breaks karaoke evening tonight, we (would tell) you more about all the great entertainment lined up for you this week.

Well, that's it, folks. If you (will have) any questions, just buzz Larry, Carrie or me, Barry, at the Paradise Club.

To show what someone said, you can either use direct or reported speech. **Direct speech** is when you put the person's exact words in quotation marks ("..."). For example: *Lee said, "I am feeling very tired."*

Reported speech is when you describe what someone said. When you do this, you change the verb into the past tense, even if the information is still true. For example: *Lee said that he was feeling very tired.*

Reporting

To put something like *Ann said, "I cooked this yesterday"* into reported speech, you drop the quotation marks* and make these changes:

> You usually add that.**

> I and you often change to he or she.

Ann said *that she* had cooked that *the day before*

> The tense of the verbs changes.

> Some expressions change.

Tenses

In reported speech, you move the tense of the verbs back into the past and change time expressions.

For example, Vicky says to Alice, "*Ian is taking his test today.*" If Alice wants to report to Debbie what Vicky has said, she should say: "*Vicky said that Ian was taking his test today.*" This applies even if Ian has not actually taken his test yet.

Here is a summary of how tenses change when verbs go into reported speech:

she ...	I said that she ...
smiles (present simple)	*smiled* (past simple)
is smiling (present continuous)	*was smiling* (past continuous)
has smiled, smiled, *had smiled* (present perfect, past simple, past perfect)	*had smiled* (past perfect)
will/would smile (future, conditional)	*would smile* (conditional)

In informal situations it is sometimes acceptable not to change the tense, when you report something that is still true (as in *Melissa said Canada is a great place to live*).

Expressions

Here you can see how some common expressions can change when they go into reported speech:

today	that day
yesterday	the day before
tomorrow	the next day
next (week)	the following (week)
last (week)/ a (week) ago	the (week) before
this (week)	that (week)
here	there
this/these	that/those

Questions and orders

To report a question (such as *Kate asked, "What are you doing?"*), you take the verb out of its question form, as well as making the usual changes. So you say *Kate asked what I was doing*, not *what was I doing*.

For questions that do not start with words like *what*, *where*, *when* or *why*, you add *if* or *whether*: *He asked if I was sick.*

When you report an order or piece of advice, you normally use the infinitive: *He told me to go home*.

As shown with these examples, with reported questions and orders, you cannot use *said* as the introducing verb. You normally use *asked* in front of a question, and *told*, *advised*, *commanded* or *warned* in front of an order.

———On the record———

Put these sentences into reported speech, following the guidelines given on this page.

1 **Liz said, "I ate Jo's chocolates yesterday."**
2 **Bobby said to us, "What did you do today?"**
3 **Carol said, "I am playing squash with my sister today."**
4 **Neil said, "Has Mandy borrowed my bike?"**
5 **The teacher said to us, "Never run across the street without looking both ways."**

*You also drop the colon (:) or comma (,) that comes in front of what is said.
**After common verbs like *say* and *tell*, you can leave *that* out: *Jo said he had cooked that the week before.*

old her   we asked   I said   Jo told her   we asked   I said

to/too

To is normally a preposition. You use it to talk about movement from one place to another (as in *I am going <u>to</u> the store*) and time (*It is five <u>to</u> three*). You use it after certain adjectives (*I am <u>responsible</u> <u>to</u> the manager*) and verbs (*He <u>looks</u> <u>forward to</u> Mondays*). *To* also makes up the infinitive of a verb, as in *<u>to</u> dream*.

Too is an adverb. You use it with other adverbs or adjectives to talk about something that is excessive (more than needed). For example: *He drives <u>too</u> fast.* *Too* is often used with *much* or *many* (*There are <u>too many</u> people*). It can also mean "as well" (*Bob is a teacher, and Shirley is <u>too</u>*).

Write this postcard out, filling the gaps with *to* or *too*.

... *Ellie,*
Having a great time here in India. Yesterday we went ... the Taj Mahal, and tomorrow we are planning ... go on a pony-trek and visit some palaces ... . We are getting used ... the heat now, but at first it just seemed ... hot ... do anything. Eating far ... many curries and spending ... much money. Anyway, it's ten ... ten and time for me ... go ... bed. Looking forward ... seeing you next week.
Much love,
Rob

The Noah C. Parker Interview

Read Noah C. Parker's interview with the soap opera star, I. MacOoldood. Then use it to write down (in full sentences) the star's replies to the questions he was asked.

Noah's natter

Mac told me that he had first decided to be a soap opera star at the age of three. He also told me that he was working on a new soap opera called Suds and Scandal, all about life at a laundromat. He said that in his spare time he did a lot of yoga and also knitted his own sweaters. And his real personality? He said he was like all celebrities - the life and soul of parties and lots of fun. Is it true, though, that his best friend is his pet rat? Mac said he had hundreds of friends, but Reginald the rat was great because he never answered back. As for travel, Mac said that he hated foreign food and having to shout to make himself understood. And his ambitions? Mac said that one day he would be the most famous person in the world.

1   When did you decide you wanted to be a soap opera star?
2   What are you working on at the moment?
3   What do you do in your spare time?
4   How would you describe your personality?
5   Is it true that your best friend is your pet rat?
6   Do you like traveling?
7   What are your ambitions?

Drama in Drabsby

Look at this report from the *Drabsby News*, and the reporter's notes on three interviews he has done. Then decide how to fill the gaps in the report. (Follow the rules on reported speech on page 24.)

Drama in Drabsby

The world-famous painting Los Forreva has been snatched from Drabsby Museum by a gang of cunning crooks. Last week's theft was discovered by curator Ivor Topjob. He said that he ..1.. at the museum at quarter past nine, and that he ..2.. at once that Los Forreva ..3.. . Extraordinarily, there appears to be no sign of any break-in. Detective B. Wildered, investigating this mysterious case, said he ..4.. so baffled by a crime, but stressed that he ..5.. into every possibility. Caretaker Luke Safteritt, who said that he ..6.. the museum as usual at half past six ..7.., insists that it was all locked up. He said that he ..8.. a door or window of the museum unlocked in all his time ..9.. . However, Ivor Topjob said that he ..10.. a few questions to ask the caretaker ..11..

Caretaker: I left the museum at half past six yesterday, as usual, and the whole place was locked and bolted. In the thirty years that I have worked here, I have never left a single door or window unlocked.

Detective B. Wildered: I have never been so baffled by a crime. When I arrived at the museum there was no sign of a break-in, yet the caretaker swears that all the doors and windows were locked. I am looking into every possibility.

Curator: I arrived at the museum at about quarter past nine, opened up, and realized at once that Los Forreva had gone. There were no broken windows or doors, though: I will have a few questions to ask the caretaker today.

Internet link: For a link to a website where you can find lots of examples of double negatives, go to **www.usborne-quicklinks.com**

Negative niggles

A **negative sentence** contains a negative word such as *not*, *nobody*, *nothing* or *never*. Be careful not to use two negative words, as this makes a sentence positive. For example: *Nobody* did *nothing* means everybody did something. The correct negative sentence is *Nobody did anything*.

When you use *not* with the infinitive of a verb (such as *to run*), it must go in front of *to*. (Otherwise you would be splitting the infinitive, see page 10.) For example: *Try* <u>not</u> *to run*.

Pronoun problems

The pronouns *it* and *you* can be subjects or objects. The others are more tricky: you use *I, he, she, we* and *they* as subjects (as in <u>*I*</u> *smiled at Jo*), but *me, him, her, us* and *them* as objects (*Jo smiled at* <u>*me*</u>). These hints will help you know which to use:

1 Use object pronouns after a preposition: *Tom is working* <u>with me</u> *today*.

2 Use subject pronouns after *as* and *than* if they are followed by a verb. For example: *I am older than* <u>*he is*</u>. When there is no verb, it is common to use object pronouns: *I am older than* <u>*him*</u>. In formal situations, though, people might say: *I am older than* <u>*he*</u>.

3 When the subject or object is two words joined by *and*, make sure you use the correct pronoun. For example: *Maria and* <u>*I*</u> (subject) *are visiting Paul*, but *Paul is visiting Maria and* <u>*me*</u> (object).

Bothers with "be"

People often use the wrong form of *to be*. For example, they say *you* <u>*was*</u> instead of *you* <u>*were*</u>. Here are the right forms:

Present simple	Past simple
I am you/we/they are he/she/it is	I was* you/we/they were he/she/it was

Trouble with "them"

Never use *them* instead of *those* in front of a noun. You should say *Pass me* <u>*those*</u> *keys*, NOT *Pass me* <u>*them*</u> *keys*.

*After *if*, it is sometimes correct to say *I were*. For example: <u>*If I were*</u> *you, I would not do that*. There is more about this on page 22.

The Supertone chair

Get rid of the mistakes in this advertisement by replacing eight words with the ones listed on the yellow note (use each once only).

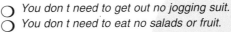

Supertone!

Ever wanted to look really great?
But not had no idea how to lose weight?
Sick of them diets and talk of fresh air?
Well, do it at home: buy a Supertone chair!

○ *You don t need to get out no jogging suit.*
○ *You don t need to eat no salads or fruit.*
○ *Just sit in your Supertone chair twice a day, and watch all them surplus pounds slip away.*
○ *You won t never have looked quite so good, that s for sure.*
○ *Nothing don t work like the Supertone cure.*
○ *Enjoy yourself, eat ice cream and cookies.*
○ *With the Supertone chair, no one has no worries.*

ever - any - your - any - those - any - those - can

Pronoun puzzler

Write out these sentences, adding one of the pronouns given in parentheses.

1 Someone has invited ... and his cousin to go to Japan. (he/him)
2 You know more about it than ... do. (I/me)
3 I hope Gary will dance with ... . (we/us)
4 Paula and ... are going out for lunch. (I/me)
5 Her brother is almost as tall as ... . (she/her)

A letter home

Write out Lucy's letter, correcting the seven mistakes she has made.

Dear Ben,
Thanks very much for the comics you sent me: they was really funny. My Dad and I went ice skating last week, and he kept falling over. I was desperately trying to not burst out laughing. My finals start next week, but I'm trying to not think about them. Otherwise I don't really have nothing to tell you. Don't forget to send me them photos you took when we was at the fair last week.
Lots of love,
Lucy

Page 3

Jumbled nouns
The unscrambled nouns are:
1 Paris (**Pisar**)   6 van (**nav**)
2 cleaners (**ranclees**)   7 dogs (**sodg**)
3 painting (**gnapinit**)   8 prison (**rosnip**)
4 policeman (**clamponie**) 9 tourists (**russitot**)
5 doors (**rodos**)

Give and take
A They had bought the **rusty** old car in **Bangkok**.
B Where is **Sarah** today?
C Outside the house stood a shiny **black bicycle**.
D I'm too **busy** to take the **dog** for a walk today.

Pages 4-5

Pronoun fillers
1 it   3 I   5 them   7 she   9 her
2 he   4 we   6 us   8 me

Identity parade
Verbs:	Nouns:	Words that can be either:
follow,	window,	scream,
undo,	desk,	study,
add,	shirt,	hope,
wander,	drawer,	fly,
write	girl	climb

1 My sister is hoping to **study** art at college.
2 We managed to **climb** up onto the ridge of the mountain.
3 Her only **hope** now is that the train is running late.
4 When the man jumped out from behind the
   door, she let out a loud **scream**.
5 Mark swatted the **fly** that kept buzzing around the room

Sentence spinner
The five sentences you can find are:
I have won a bronze medal.
It was following the young girl.
We are catching an early plane.
They bought a black dog.
She knows the tall man.
It was following the young girl still makes sense when
the object and subject are swapped over: *The young girl
was following it.*

A sack of words
Nouns: postcard, song, Louise, computer, beauty
Verbs: will buy, to cry, is working, to dream, waited
Adjectives: unhappy, sunny, loud
Pronouns: she, we, they, you
Articles: an, the, a

affect/effect
Affect is a verb. *Effect* is usually a noun.
1 What is the **effect** of adding flour to water?
2 That movie was really good. There were lots of
   special **effects**.
3 I had a cold, but it didn't really **affect** me very badly.
4 Her illness had a very bad **effect** on her test results.
5 The weather can **affect** the way you feel.

Pages 6-7

Scrambled - after, between, across, into, under
1 My car was parked **between** the truck and
   the motorcycle.
2 They walked home **after** the party.
3 The dog jumped **into** the lake.
4 The prisoner ran as fast as he could **across** the bridge.
5 The money was hidden **under** the bed.

Sentence building
He couldn't remember her name, **although** he had
met her before.
He forced the door open **and** crept quietly into the
house.
Michelle rushed to the window and looked for the car,
but it had already gone.
I can't play tennis today **because** my knee hurts.
She listened to music on her headphones **while** she
was jogging.

Sentence parts
1 The / dog / ran / into / the / road /
   and / the / car / just / missed / it.
2 We / are having / a / big / party, / so /
   you / must come.
3 The / big / bear / escaped / from / the /
   zoo / and / was / never / seen / again.
4 The / dancers / were / so / shocked /
   they / had to stop / the / show.

borrow/lend; teach/learn

Fill the gap
1	muddy	6	creaky	11	cheerful
2	loud	7	lightly	12	merrily
3	quietly	8	faint	13	thankfully
4	empty	9	deeply		
5	heavily	10	suddenly		

Pages 8-9

Sentence splitting
Here you can see where you should have broken up the
sentences (losing *but* and *and*):
... for the past three **weeks**. **She** refused to ...
... with chips and soda **pop**. **They** don't get ...

Clause spotting

Main clauses: She phoned the police/They arrived/my friend kept a stick insect/One day he let it out
Subordinate clauses: which squashed the poor stick insect/which had incredibly long legs/while Mrs. Kettani was in her yard/because she was terrified of large insects
Phrases: in a fast car/In the house next door/in a panic/in the street

In the house next door, my friend kept a stick insect which had incredibly long legs. One day he let it out in the street while Mrs. Kettani was in her yard. She phoned the police in a panic because she was terrified of large insects. They arrived in a fast car which squashed the poor stick insect.

Sentence stretch

Here are some examples of the most likely extended sentences.

1 The **hungry** monkey **greedily** ate six bananas **when the zookeeper had gone**.
2 She **often** eats at the **Chinese** restaurant **where her brother is a waiter**.
3 He **stupidly** drove the **new** car into a ditch, **because he was fiddling with the radio**.
4 Joanna **slowly** walked up to the **young** horse **which had thrown her off its back**.

an/a

1 He gave me **a** used railway ticket.
2 Jill said she had seen **a** UFO.
3 They gave her **an** X-ray and said she'd be fine.
4 From his window he has **an** incredible view over New York.
5 This is **a** one-way street.
6 Sometimes, a friend can turn into **an** enemy.
7 It was such **a** hot day.
8 It was **an** honest answer.
9 He has **an** older brother.

Picture puzzlers

The sentences that match the pictures on the left are:
1 The girl with the dog gave the envelope to the man.
2 The man who was wearing blue beat his rival.
3 The plant was in the corner of the room with the yellow flowers.
4 Jane rested her foot, which was shaking, on the top rung of the ladder.

The sentences that match the pictures on the right are:
1 The girl gave the envelope to the man with the dog.
2 The man beat his rival, who was wearing blue.
3 The plant with the yellow flowers was in the corner of the room.
4 Jane rested her foot on the top rung of the ladder, which was shaking.

Adverb adding

1A He's **just** told me I will have to take it easy for a few days.
1B He's told me I will **just** have to take it easy for a few days.
1C He's told me I will have to take it easy **just** for a few days or for **just** a few days.
2A There were **only** a few chocolates left, but Sue ate two.
2B There were a few chocolates left, but Sue **only** ate two.
2C There were a few chocolates left, but **only** Sue ate two.

their/they're/there

1 There **are seven people** in a netball team.
2 Their **dog is** outside.
3 They're **still** in the swimming pool.
4 Their **lawyer is on his** way.
5 Isn't she there **any more**?
6 They're **away** on vacation.

Pages 10-11

Splitting up

You can finish all the food in the freezer, except for the chocolate cake I made for Dad's birthday, and the leg of lamb, which I'd like you **to take out on Saturday**, please. Also, before Mr. Hopkins drops by on Wednesday, I'd like you **to vacuum the sitting room thoroughly**. Could you remember **to water the tomatoes regularly**? By the way, I told Mary you'd try **to drop in on her quickly**.
Before you go out, remember **to double-lock the door carefully**.
Please don't forget to put Bingo out before you go to bed. You need **to feed my goldfish every night**. See you on Saturday - we're going **to try to get the afternoon train if possible**. Perhaps you could pick us up from the station if we give you a call?

Pages 12-13

Island mission

Here you can see what Ivor Cunningplan's instructions say when they are pieced together:
Your mission is to deliver the Silicon documents to the leader of the Sneak Street gang.
First go to the islands of Skee-ming, which lie in the Wylin Ocean. Then head for the city of Ska-lee-wags, which is on the northernmost island. Once there, you will easily locate Sneak Street.
On Friday night, five members of the gang are meeting on the corner of Sneak Street. Each member knows that the documents are being delivered by a man with a limp. Walk up to the gang. If someone says: "Here come Art Fulfox and his dog," then it is not safe to deliver the documents. If someone says: "Here comes Art Fulfox," you can drop them off and return to HQ.

Beach breaks

You will take exit C.

The matched-up sentences you will make are:

The sausages and chicken are on the barbecue.

A few of the gang were playing volleyball.

Everyone was enjoying themselves.

A box of sandwiches was lying in the sand.

One of our comics was blowing into the sea.

My shorts were covered in chocolate.

Each of them has bought a different ice cream.

Catherine and her sister are here.

Many people are in the sea.

off/of

Sentences 1, 3, 4 and 6 are missing *of*.

Sentences 2, 5 and 7 are missing *off*.

Fill the gaps

1   There **were** layers of dust on the piano.

2   "Here **are** Ann and Graham!" she shrieked, pointing across the street.

3   A little bit of money **goes** a long way.

4   When we got back, there **was** a bucketful of tomatoes on the doorstep.

5   Most motorcycles are cheaper than cars and **go** much faster.

6   Success **is** more important to him than happiness.

Pages 14-15

like/as

They left school at four o'clock, as usual.

The city was just **as** it had always been.

Andy looks **like** my cousin.

Rachael's dog was **like** a large black sheep.

Her head felt **as if** it was about to explode.

After her illness, she looked **like** an old lady.

Tense trippers

Monday

Just before lunch Stuart got a flat tire. No one had a flat tire repair kit, so we **had** to walk miles to the nearest town. When we finally got there, someone directed us to a bike shop, so we **went** all the way there and then **found** it was closed.

Tuesday

The day went well until we **got** caught behind a herd of sheep on a narrow lane. It took us two hours to get past them, so by the time we got to the youth hostel, it **was** completely full.

Wednesday

Stopped for lunch in a little village. Left our bikes by the church, went to a café, and when we **came** out, Sheila's bike **had** disappeared. Then suddenly we spotted the local priest riding the missing bike, so we **flagged** him down and he explained everything. The poor priest sold his own bike a year ago, but he keeps forgetting, so every time he sees a black bike he **thinks** it's his.

Thursday

Arrived at the station to get the train home. We loaded our bikes on board and then **went** for coffee while we **were** waiting. Suddenly, Stuart noticed that the train was leaving! We **had put** OR We'd **put** our bikes on the wrong one!

Which is which?

have crashed   will understand   invaded

smiled   did not arrive   sing

had promised   buys   had painted

sit   has spotted

had visited   will drive

Getting snappy

The photos should be arranged in this order:

Caption A: 1, 2, 3

Caption B: 3, 1, 2

Caption C: 2, 1, 3

Caption D: 2, 3, 1

Pages 16-17

Lost for words

Andrew's desk

He has blown out the candle.

He has broken a glass.

He has eaten an apple.

He has written a letter.

In the afternoon, he blew out the candle.

In the afternoon, he broke a glass.

In the afternoon, he ate an apple.

In the afternoon, he wrote a letter.

Tense trouble

1   They will have to pick up the house before their parents **get back**.

2   Oliver had just finished writing when the examiner **told** them to put down their pens.

3   Lots of people **will visit** the exhibition when it opens next month.

4   I was furious because the train **was** late.

5   She **went** to Hong Kong last year.

6   They **have lived** in New York for two years, and have no plans to move away.

can/may/might

1   I am very glad that Jenny **can** speak French.

2   You **can** spend as much money as you like OR You **may** spend as much money as you like.

3   **Can** I borrow a pencil? OR **May** I borrow a pencil?

4   **May** I phone my parents? OR **Might** I phone my parents?

5   I **might** go and see a movie this afternoon, if it keeps on raining OR I **may** go and see a movie this afternoon, if it keeps on raining.

Pages 18-19

Identity crisis
1 The fridge is full of bacon. (**which I eat everyday**)
2 The ring which he gave me was far too big.
3 The policeman who drove them home was very friendly.
4 My brother is getting married. (**who is a vet**)
5 The boat had been underwater for thirty years. (**which was found by a diver**)

Who or *whom*?
1 The friend with **whom** I went to Egypt has sent me a letter.
2 The people **who** took the other path got there first.
3 Valerie, **who** has just come back from Mexico, speaks fluent Spanish.
4 This is Jo, **whom** I met on the bus OR **who** I met on the bus.

Murder at Snoot Towers
1	which	4	who	7	which
2	who	5	whom	8	whom/that
3	that/which	6	whose	9	that

Hugo Batty murdered Lord Snoot, whom he was blackmailing. Here you can see how he managed to slip unnoticed from the library to the conservatory, by going through the gardens, the nursery and the breakfast room:

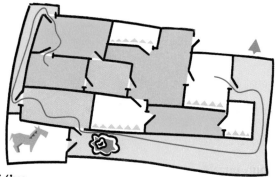

Of/'ve
1 "She **must've** decided not to take her car, because I saw it parked in our street this morning."
2 "You really **should've** gone to the party: it was great fun."
3 "We **could've** driven a bit faster, but not much, as the roads are very wet."
4 "If it hadn't been raining, I **would've** come."

Who's who and what's what?
1 The girl **who is swimming** is near the boat.
2 The dog **which is running** has black paws.
3 The ice cream **which the boy is holding** is chocolate and vanilla.
4 The boy **who is running** has red hair.
5 The cow **the policeman is chasing** has black ears.
6 The dog **which is swimming** is near the boat.
7 The baby **the woman is holding** has a pink hat.
8 The man **whom the policeman is chasing** has a red sweater.

Pages 20-21

Comparing climates
1 In August, Weatherchester is **hotter** than Seasonbury.
2 In January, Weatherchester is **colder** than Seasonbury.
3 In March, Seasonbury is **drier** than Weatherchester.
4 In September, Seasonbury is **wetter** than Weatherchester.

Character questionnaire
Jon is more patient than Tessa.
Jon is lazier than Tessa.
Tessa is friendlier than Jon.
Jon is more careful than Tessa.
Tessa is nosier than Jon.
Jon is more selfish than Tessa.

Quite/quiet
1 You look **quite** washed out.
2 As Stefan walked **past**, he noticed the man's gun.
3 It is very **quiet** without Diane and Vicky.
4 Veronica was so happy when she **passed** her test.
5 In the **past** week, I have lost two umbrellas.
6 I have always found math **quite** hard.

Moped mania
The Superwhizz is wider than the Pipsqueak.
The Superwhizz is longer than the Pipsqueak.
The Superwhizz is more expensive than the Pipsqueak.
The Superwhizz is faster than the Pipsqueak.
The Superwhizz is heavier than the Pipsqueak.
The Stumbly is wider than the Featherzoom.
The Featherzoom is longer than the Stumbly.
The Featherzoom is more expensive than the Stumbly.
The Featherzoom is faster than the Stumbly.
The Stumbly is heavier than the Featherzoom.
The Thriftyshift is wider than the Pipsqueak.
The Thriftyshift is longer than the Pipsqueak.
The Pipsqueak is more expensive than the Thriftyshift.
The Pipsqueak is faster than the Thriftyshift.
The Pipsqueak is heavier than the Thriftyshift.
The fastest moped Sally can buy is a Pipsqueak.

The Superwhizz is too expensive and the Feathezoom is too long.

Pages 22-23

in/into
1 He could see a girl diving **into** the pool.
2 Elaine hurried **into** her bedroom.
3 The train had been waiting **in** the tunnel for more than half an hour.
4 We went **into** the garden to look for worms.
5 I lay **in** the bathtub for forty minutes today.